ESSENTIAL OILS FOR YOUR DOG:
30 RECIPES THAT WILL KEEP YOUR DOG HEALTHY

Copyright © 2015 by Shehan Peiris

All rights reserved. This book or any portion thereof may not be reproduced or used in any manner whatsoever without the express written permission of the publisher except for the use of brief quotations in a book review or scholarly journal.

First Printing: 2015

Disclaimer

This book is not intended as a substitute for the medical advice of veterinarians. The reader should regularly consult a veterinary doctor in matters relating to his/her pet's health and particularly with respect to any symptoms that may require diagnosis or medical attention.

Contents
INTRODUCTION 3
UNDERSTANDING THE BENEFITS OF TRUE, HOLISTIC ESSENTIAL OILS 4
UNDERSTANDING CARRIER OILS 6
SAFE ESSENTIAL OILS FOR YOUR DOG 8
ESSENTIAL OIL APPLICATION TECHNIQUES FOR DOGS....................................12
HOW TO BLEND ESSENTIAL OILS FOR DOGS..13
THIRTY ESSENTIAL OIL BLENDS YOU CAN CREATE FOR YOUR DOG..................15

INTRODUCTION

Essential oils are volatile substances obtained from fruit, seeds, barks, roots, leaves or stem of a plant through the process of carbon dioxide extraction, steam distillation, manual expression or solvent extraction. They are highly aromatic and extremely concentrated. This is the reason why almost all essential oils are recommended to be diluted prior to usage.

It is also important to understand that all plants do not produce essential oils.

Understanding essential oils also implies that we understand carrier oils, hydrosols and absolutes.

Hydrosols are water based substances that are a by-product of steam distillation of essential oils. They contain the water soluble parts of the plant along with trace amounts of essential oil components. All essential oils do not produce hydrosols. This is because all essential oils are not manufactured through the process of steam distillation.

Carrier oils are the oils that are used to dilute essential oils prior to topical use. They are extracted from the fatty portion of the plant, usually from kernels, seeds or nuts.

Absolutes are highly aromatic liquids that are extracted from plants using certain complex chemical solvents that are usually removed during the final phase of creation.

But you understand essential oils already and use them every day?

Yup, the banana coat conditioner for you dog has some essential oils. It is labelled as 'aroma therapeutic,' isn't it?

Well, this is a misconception a number of pet lovers suffer from.

If you've ever visited an aromatherapy pharmacy or a pet store, you would have noticed a number of products labelled as *'for use in aromatherapy'*, or *'aroma therapeutic.'*

It is important to understand that all these products may not be truly aroma therapeutic.

So, why do they smell like fruit?

Simple – because like you, a number of consumers believe that these fruity fragrances are all natural. You must understand that most of these fruity fragrances are false aromatherapy products. They are synthesized in the laboratory through the use of synthetic 'fragrance oils.'

UNDERSTANDING THE BENEFITS OF TRUE, HOLISTIC ESSENTIAL OILS

A true, holistic essential oil is completely natural and is generally created to positively influence the physical and emotional health of an animal or a human. How these oils smell does not matter, all that matters is the manner in which they are used in aromatherapy. An example worth mentioning here would be the essential oil of the plant, Helichrysum italicum. It smells awful, but its uses in treating your pets are phenomenal.

Therefore, it becomes extremely important to understand that sometimes you must put aside the appealing aspect of essential oils and only focus on the tremendous potential they offer.

Let us look at some of the benefits that these essential oils have to offer:

- Essential oils are easy to use and super convenient.
- They are organic and natural – so your pet gets the best benefits from Mother Earth.
- They can be diluted with ease.
- They can relieve aches and pains in a pet.
- They are great at solving any problems related to digestion in the pet.
- Minor cuts, injuries, wounds, itches, etc. are almost immediately relieved through proper use of essential oils.
- They are rich in anti-oxidants and provide a boost to the immune system.
- They can calm the pet and in the process elevate the general well being too.
- Some of them smell great and your pet loves them!

Here are some common dog ailments where essential oils can work wonders:

- Allergies
- Burns
- Bad breath
- Anxiety
- Insomnia
- Cuts
- Cracked paw pads
- Fatigue
- Dirty ears
- General detoxification
- Deodorizing
- Fear
- Gastritis
- Flatulence
- Hyper-sexuality
- Hyperacidity
- Flea infestations

- Ticks
- Itchy skin
- Infected ears
- Motion sickness
- Unhealthy coat
- Skin infections
- Teething pain
- Weak immune system

And here is the list of some essential oils that should **never** be used with pets:

- Bitter Almond
- Camphor
- Cassia
- Boldo
- Anise
- Birch
- Calamus
- Lavender
- Mustard
- Mugwort
- Clove leaf and bud
- Garlic
- Juniper (use Juniper berry only)
- Pennyroyal
- Oregano
- White or red Thyme
- Wintergreen
- Yarrow
- Wormwood
- Thuja
- Rue

UNDERSTANDING CARRIER OILS

Base oils or carrier oils are the oils used to dilute essential oils. They are extracted through a number of methods, the most common being cold pressing and solvent extraction. Cold pressed oils are always preferred.

A number of animal lovers stay away from base oils- they do not want to apply these oils to the fur or coat of their animal assuming that this will attract dirt. This is however a misconception.

It is important to understand that natural vegetable and nut based oils do not cause any grease or dirt, and can be easily absorbed through the skin. Petroleum jelly and mineral oils contribute to dirt and grease.

Some base oils that can be used for diluting essential oils or use in pets are:

- Coconut oil
- Castor oil
- Avocado oil
- Apricot Kernel oil
- Sweet Almond oil
- Sesame oil
- Olive oil
- Sunflower Seed oil
- Rosehip Seed oil
- Jojoba oil
- Hazelnut oil

In your pursuit for administering holistic aroma-therapeutic products to your pets, you may begin to use other botanical ingredients too. These can include solid butters such as cocoa or mango or even beeswax. The possibilities are endless...

Here are some other helpful products that you may need as you decide to prepare the best essential oil blends for your pet:

Herbs: You must work with organically grown herbs whenever possible. Herbs are used in herbal rinses for grooming your pet or for infusing your carrier oils. The best way to incorporate herbs into your essential oils kit is by growing your own herbs.

Butters: Mango butter, shea butter, cocoa butter – all elevate the therapeutic and moisturizing capability of your blend. It is important to be extremely sure that you are using unrefined butters only.

Clays: Clays are used to prepare poultices (that are created by blending essential oils and herbs). French clays are considered as the best for pets.

Waxes: Waxes find the most common use in creation of soothing balms and ointments. Only unrefined, unbleached waxes are recommended. Beeswax is the most commonly used wax.

Aloe Vera: The best way to use this soothing ingredient is by keeping the leaves on the hand and applying directly. If you are buying Aloe Vera from a commercial supplier, make sure that it is preservative free.

Alcohols: Natural alcohols are extremely important since essential oils do not mix with water. If you need to use alcohol, use grain alcohol only.

Flower essences: Natural flower essences are added to a number of essential oil blends in order to elevate the synergistic impact of the formulation. You must stay away from synthetic blends though.

Gemstone essences: Gemstone essences, that form a part of energy healing are absolutely safe and pose no side effects.

Shampoos and soaps: A number of pet lovers today try and prepare their own soaps. Soaps can be prepared in two ways: through cold pressing and through the use of glycerin. Glycerin soaps are fun and simple to make. However, most of them use petrochemicals that are not recommended for your pet. Cold pressed soaps are better and 100% natural.

Do not wash your pet with commercially available soaps and shampoos. They are full of synthetic products and fragrances that may actually harm your pet. A number of pet lovers are tempted to add some essential oils to liquid soaps in order to prepare a quick pet shampoo. This is not recommended, because unnatural products (chemicals) used in the liquid soap may strip the animal of moisture. An ingredient called 'decyl polyglucose' can be used to prepare an extraordinary gentle soap for pets. The process to prepare this has been explained later in the book.

SAFE ESSENTIAL OILS FOR YOUR DOG

Here are the top fifteen essential oils that can safely be used for your dogs:

ESSENTIAL OIL ONE: CARROT SEED ESSENTIAL OIL (*Daucus carota*)

The carrot seed essential oil is a valuable oil that can be used for skin care, especially in animals who have flaky, dry and allergy prone skin. The oil, although extracted from the seeds of the carrot plant, does not smell like the carrot itself. It is also not extracted from the orange colored carrots that you get in the supermarket.

The source of this oil is a wild carrot (Called the Queen Anne's Lace).

The seed oil possesses a distinct scent that is nutty, warm, herbal and immensely earthy at the same time.

This extraordinarily gentle oil has minimal side effects and is capable of boosting tissue regeneration and rejuvenation.

ESSENTIAL OIL TWO: SWEET MARJORAM ESSENTIAL OIL (*Origanum marjorana*)

The Sweet Marjoram Essential oil has a calming fragrance that soothes the central nervous system. It demonstrates an antibacterial, calming and spasmolytic effect. It is used in combination with other grounding essential oils. It is also used as an insect repellant or for wound care and skin infections.

ESSENTIAL OIL THREE: GERMAN CHAMOMILE ESSENTIAL OIL (*Matricaria recutita*)

The German chamomile essential oil is one of the most powerful, anti-inflammatory, skin soothing essential oil. The skin soothing action of this oil is due to the presence of chamazulene, a sesquiterpene hydrocarbon responsible for the deep, indigo color of this oil. It is great for use on skin irritations, burns and allergies. An important point to be noted here is that owing to its gentle nature, this oil is used in an undiluted form in humans. This should, however, never be done in animals.

Animals have an extremely sensitive nose. Therefore, we must ensure that the oil that we use is extraordinarily gentle.

ESSENTIAL OIL FOUR: ROMAN CHAMOMILE ESSENTIAL OIL (*Anthemis nobilis*)

The Roman Chamomile essential oil possesses a strong analgesic action, which make it extremely useful for tooth ache and wound care. The antispasmodic and calming esters present in the oil relieve muscle pains, cramps, etc. and soothe the central nervous system. It is non-toxic and extremely gentle with a very intense fragrance. Although it is extremely harmless, you must always dilute it prior to use. It is also one of the costlier essential oils.

ESSENTIAL OIL FIVE: CEDARWOOD ESSENTIAL OIL (*Cedrus Atlantica*)

The Cedarwood essential oil elevates circulation and boosts the release of toxins. Humans use this essential oil for cellulite reduction. However, this is not the recommended reason for usage in dogs.

The circulation boosting impact of this oil makes it extremely great for usage in cases of dermatitis in dogs. It is also used in conditioning blends for the skin.

Fleas do not like this oil and therefore stay away from the animal if it is applied on the skin. Use it in any flea repellant blend to experience the miraculous benefits.

Cedarwood essential oil also demonstrates a moderate antiseptic effect, diminishes congestion in the lymphatic and circulatory system and tones the animal's skin.

ESSENTIAL OIL SIX: CLARY SAGE ESSENTIAL OIL (*Salvia sclarea*)

The clary sage essential oil is one of the gentlest essential oils with presence of calming esters that can sedate the central nervous system. This makes it a welcome addition to any essential oil blend.

ESSENTIAL OIL SEVEN: EUCALYPTUS ESSENTIAL OIL (Eucalyptus radiata)

The Eucalyptus essential oil is well tolerated and easily metabolized. It is a gentle oil which works very well in cases of congestion. It possesses some amazing anti-inflammatory, antiviral and expectorant properties. It makes an excellence deodorizer and flea repellant too!

An important point to note here is that this oil acts as an antidote in homeopathic treatments. Therefore, you must avoid using it if your dog is availing homeopathic treatment.

ESSENTIAL OIL EIGHT: GINGER ESSENTIAL OIL (Zingiber officinale)

The Ginger Essential Oil is deceptive, it does not taste like ginger! It is economical to use and acts as a wonderful addition to blends that are used to cure motion sickness for dogs. It is a great digestive and can be used in pets to manage hyperacidity, flatulence, etc. It is a great massage aid and acts an amazing additive to massage blends for dogs suffering from dysplasia, sprains or arthritis. It is non-irritating, non-toxic and extremely safe to use.

ESSENTIAL OIL NINE: GERANIUM ESSENTIAL OIL (Pelargonium graveolens)

The Geranium essential oil boasts of an extremely soft, pleasant and floral aroma with a Rose overtone. It is priced at a reasonable rate and has strong antifungal effects. It also works as an excellent toner. It is used in skin ailments and treatment of fungal infections in the dog's ears. It is also a pesticide free, eco-friendly and safe dog repellant

ESSENTIAL OIL TEN: HELICHRYSUM ESSENTIAL OIL (*Helichrysum italicum*)

The Helichrysum essential oil has often been called the most amazing essential oil available for pets. The regenerative, analgesic and anti-inflammatory properties of this oil are attributed to the presence of calming esters in it. It must be diluted prior to each use and is extremely effective for use in all pets.

ESSENTIAL OIL ELEVEN: MANDARIN GREEN ESSENTIAL OIL (*Citrus reticulata*)

The Green Mandarin Essential oil is the sweetest of all citrus essential oils. It is an excellent addition to essential oil blends used to diminish anxiety, fear or insomnia. The pleasant fragrance and calming properties make it the essential oil of choice for pets.

The oil possesses photosynthesizing properties. Therefore, direct exposure to sun post the application of this oil should be avoided. Most animals possess a furry coat to protect themselves. However, this warning is definitely valid for certain breeds of hairless dogs.

ESSENTIAL OIL TWELVE: LAVENDER ESSENTIAL OIL (*Lavandula angustifolia*)

Lavender is the most well-known essential oil. Along with its gentleness and pleasing scent, Lavender offers a range of therapeutic benefits. It can be blended with other essential oils to soothe skin ailments, or provide the animal with generalized healing and first aid.

The Lavender essential oil has anti-pruritic, anti-bacterial and amazing regenerative properties. The calming effect of Lavender can be boosted further by blending it with other calming essential oils.

ESSENTIAL OIL THIRTEEN: MYRRH ESSENTIAL OIL (*Commiphora myrrha*)

Boasting of a warm, deep and earthy fragrance, the myrrh essential oil is known for its anti-inflammatory properties. It also possesses some amazing anti-viral properties. In dogs, it is primarily used to ease teething pain or treating skin inflammation. It is also used in immune system blends. Myrrh is also an important essential oil that can be used in tick repellant blends.

ESSENTIAL OIL FOURTEEN: NIAOULI ESSENTIAL OIL *(Melaleuca, quinquenervia, viridiflora)*

The Niaouli essential oil is pretty much similar to Tea Tree essential oil. It is, however, preferred to the Tea Tree oil owing to tis pleasant aroma and anti-inflammatory and antihistaminic properties. It is a powerful antibacterial too. It is often referred to as 'MQV.

ESSENTIAL OIL FIFTEEN: ROMAN CHAMOMILE ESSENTIAL OIL (*Chamaemelum nobile*)

An absolute essential in your cabinet, this oil works wonders on the central nervous system and helps in teething pains, joint aches and soothing the nerves.

ESSENTIAL OIL APPLICATION TECHNIQUES FOR DOGS

There are three basic methods to use essential oil on your dog. Correct dilution and application ensures that you do not harm your pet and that they reap maximum benefits.

The three techniques are:

Topical application: A topical application implies that the oil should be applied to the skin directly. It is a super effective method as the oil begins to work quickly and efficiently right from the moment it is applied. The main advantage of this method is that it allows to you monitor the amount of oil that is being used as opposed to inhalation where you would not be sure of how much your dog has inhaled.

You could apply the oil (diluted of course) directly by massaging over the impacted area. It could also be sprayed on to the skin of your pet post dilution via spray bottle.

It could be mixed with balms, ointments, or shampoos too.

Diffusion: This method incorporates diffusion of oil in the air with the help of a diffuser. This oil is then inhaled by the dog. The diffuser must be allowed to run for at least forty minutes at a stretch. This will give the dog enough time to inhale it. A one week therapy can show visible results.

Oral application: In this method, the oil is given to the dog for ingestion. The dose must be carefully chosen as essential oils are extremely concentrated and can cause harm, if used undiluted.

HOW TO BLEND ESSENTIAL OILS FOR DOGS

Dogs are much more sensitive to essential oils than humans. The reason for this is the sharper sense of smell which they possess. It is therefore, extremely important to dilute essential oils prior to use.

The size of the pet is another point of consideration. Most dogs are smaller in size than humans. This implies that the dosage administered to them and the manner in which the essential oil to be used is diluted varies for dogs and humans.

Before we move further, let me explain the difference between dosage and dilution.

The word '*dosage*' when used in context of essential oils refers to the amount of final formulation that is used with the animal. This is generally expressed in terms of 'spritzes', 'drops', etc.

On the other hand, the word '*dilution*' means the quantity of essential oil present in a particular formulation.

A number of safety measures need to be considered before blending or using essential oils for dogs.

Some of these are listed below:

- Only highest quality essential oils that are sourced from a reliable vendor should be used to create a blend.
- Essential oils for pets should never be blended with other synthetic ingredients such as laundry detergents, dishwashing soaps, or human shampoos that are not 100% natural.
- They should be stored in dark colored glass bottles only.
- Dilution is a must. It is one of the most important steps in the process of using essential oils. You must begin with 25% of human dose. This would translate to ten drops of essential oil to ½ oz. of base oil, or thirty drops of essential oil in 8oz. of shampoo or any other base. This would mean 2% of the final volume of the preparation.
- You must not rely on a single essential oil for best results. Essential oils are more impactful when used synergistically with one another. Blending a few essential oils and hydrosols together can elevate the therapeutic benefits of the oils.
- A dog should never be exposed to essential oils that are rich in phenols and ketones. Most of these are toxic. The list of essential oils to be avoided has been provided in the earlier chapter of this book.
- Internal administration should be avoided. Only use an essential oil internally if the recipe demands and ensure that you are diluting the oil to the maximum. Remember the principle of 'less is more.'
- Try and avoid using essential oils on puppies younger than ten weeks. When you introduce your puppy to essential oils, begin with the smallest possible amount. And

if you are in doubt, begin with hydrosols. They are the safest option. Don't forget to dilute them though!
- Dogs must be introduced to essential oils in a gradual manner. You must watch out for any physical symptoms. Letting the dog smell the oil before use or using very little of it diminishes side effects such as panting, whining or drooling.
- Take the size of your dog into consideration while administering essential oils to them. This means that small dogs will generally respond with low dosage and large dogs may need a higher dose of the same essential oil.
- Take special precautions while creating blends if your dog is epileptic or prone to seizures. Calming essential oils have a positive impact on these pets as they sedate the central nervous system. Certain oils, on the other hand, can trigger the onset of seizures. Rosemary essential oil is one such oil.
- Essential oils should never be used near or close to genital areas, anus, eyes or nose of your dog.
- A pipette should be used to dispense essential oil drops to your dog.
- Shake all essential oil blends before use. This is because essential oils and water do not mix.
- Try and discourage ingestion of essential oils. However, do not panic if your dog accidently licks some from his fur. After all, you are using really diluted and safe essential oils, aren't you?
- Your dog will not be able to tell you how it feels. You must observe for all the subtle signs that it provides to you.

THIRTY ESSENTIAL OIL BLENDS YOU CAN CREATE FOR YOUR DOG

BLEND ONE FOR ANXIETY:

- 15 ml. of carrier oil (e.g. sweet almond oil, olive oil, jojoba oil)
- 4 drops Valerian
- 6 drops Lavender
- 3 drops Clary Sage
- 4 drops Sweet Marjoram

This blend must be used topically. You can rub four drops of this blend between your hands and then apply it on your dog's ears, under their armpits and between the thighs.

BLEND TWO FOR CALMING YOUR DOG:

- 5 parts of Lavender
- 3 parts of Bergamot
- 2 parts of Melissa
- 2 parts of Ylang Ylang

Mix fifteen drops of this oil in one cup of baking soda. Stir and shake well before use.

BLEND THREE FOR ARTHRITIS:

- 15 ml. of base oil (e.g. sweet almond oil, olive oil, jojoba oil)
- 8 drops Helichrysum
- 5 drops Peppermint
- 2 drops Ginger
- 3 drops Valerian

Use this blend to massage your dog's sore joints. You can even apply some oil on the inside of their ears.

BLEND FOUR FOR ARTHRITIS:

- 15 ml. of base oil (e.g. sweet almond oil, olive oil, jojoba oil)
- 6 drops Rosemary oil
- 3 drops Lavender
- 4 drops Ginger

Use this blend to massage your dog's sore joints. You can even apply some oil on the inside of their ears.

BLEND FIVE FOR BAD ODOR:

- 3 drops Roman Chamomile
- 3 drops Geranium
- 10 drops Lavender
- 4 drops Sweet Marjoram

Mix the above blend with an all-natural shampoo (recipe provided in the book).

BLEND SIX FOR RAINY DAY DOG ODOR

- 12 drops Lavender
- 8 drops Sweet Orange
- 6 drops Peppermint
- 4 drops Eucalyptus

Combine these together in a spray bottle and spray on your dog's body. Make sure that you do not spray on their face.

BLEND SEVEN FOR EAR INFECTION

- 15 ml. of base oil (e.g. sweet almond oil, olive oil, jojoba oil)
- 8 drops Lavender
- 4 drops Tea tree or Niaouli
- 8 drops Bergamot
- 4 drops Roman Chamomile

Mix these together in a dark colored bottle and use a dropper to dip a few drops into your dog's ear when infected.

BLEND EIGHT FOR EAR INFECTION

- 15 ml. of base oil (e.g. sweet almond oil, olive oil, jojoba oil)
- 8 drops Lavender
- 4 drops Tea tree or Niaouli
- 4 drops Peppermint

Mix these together in a dark colored bottle and use a dropper to dip a few drops into your dog's ear when infected.

BLEND NINE FOR TREATING WOUNDS

- 15 ml. of base oil (e.g. sweet almond oil, olive oil, jojoba oil)
- 8 drops Lavender
- 4 drop Helichrysum
- 6 drops Marjoram, Sweet
- 4 drops Niaouli

This blend is handy for minor bruises, cuts, wounds and insect bites.

BLEND TEN FOR TREATING FLEAS

- 20 ml. of base oil (e.g. sweet almond oil, olive oil, jojoba oil)
- 4 drops Citronella
- 6 drops Lemon
- 6 drops Clary Sage
- 10 drops of Peppermint

Use this blend over your dog's neck, legs, tail, back and chest. You may even want to add a few drops to their collar.

BLEND ELEVEN FOR TREATING FLEAS

- 20 ml. of base oil (e.g. sweet almond oil, olive oil, jojoba oil)
- 4 drops Palo Santo
- 6 drops Lemongrass
- 6 drops Lavender

Use this blend over your dog's neck, legs, tail, back and chest. You may even want to add a few drops to their collar.

BLEND TWELVE FOR CALMING YOUR HYPERACTIVE DOG

- 20 ml. of base oil (e.g. sweet almond oil, olive oil, jojoba oil)
- 6 drops Valerian
- 4 drops Lavender
- 2 drops Chamomile, Roman
- 4 drops Sweet Marjoram
- 4 drops Bergamot

This blend must be used topically. You can rub four drops of this blend between your hands and then apply it on your dog's ears, under their armpits and between the thighs.

BLEND THIRTEEN FOR SKIN ALLERGIES

- 20 ml. of base oil (e.g. sweet almond oil, olive oil, jojoba oil)
- 10 drops Lavender
- 5 drops Geranium
- 6 drops Chamomile, German
- 2 drops Carrot Seed

Use this blend topically. You can rub four drops of this blend between your hands and then apply it on your dog's ears, under their armpits and between the thighs.

BLEND FOURTEEN AS A MOSQUITO REPELLANT

- 30 drops of Citronella
- 12 drops of Lemongrass
- 12 drops of Rose Geranium
- 12 drops of Myrrh
- 10 ounces of Aloe Vera juice

Spray this over your dog's coat, carefully avoiding the eye area.

BLEND FIFTEEN FOR MOTION SICKNESS

- 20 ml. of base oil (e.g. sweet almond oil, olive oil, jojoba oil)
- 8 drops of Ginger
- 12 drops of Peppermint

Apply this blend on your dog's ears, coat, thighs and armpits.

BLEND FIFTEEN FOR SINUS INFECTION

- 20 ml. of base oil (e.g. sweet almond oil, olive oil, jojoba oil)
- 10 drops of Eucalyptus
- 6 drops of Myrhh
- 8 drops of Ravensare

You can massage this blend into the fur of your dog's neck and chest. You can also add this blend into a diffuser and let your dog experience it for around ten minutes four times a day.

BLEND SIXTEEN FOR TICKS

- 20 ml. of base oil (e.g. sweet almond oil, olive oil, jojoba oil)
- 10 drops Lavender
- 8 drops Geranium
- 6 drops Bay Leaf

In order to use, apply this blend over your dog's neck, tail and feet.

BLEND SEVENTEEN FOR TICKS

- 20 ml. of base oil (e.g. sweet almond oil, olive oil, jojoba oil)
- 10 drops Rosewood
- 8 drops Geranium
- 6 drops Myrrh

In order to use, apply this blend over your dog's neck, tail and feet.

BLEND EIGHTEEN PUPPY SHAMPOO

- 10 drops Geranium
- 5 drops Ylang Ylang
- 8 drops Petitgrain
- 8 drops Rose

The above blend must be added to eight ounce all natural shampoo (recipe provided later in the book).

BLEND NINETEEN TO FRESHEN UP FOR PUPPY

- 20 ml. Olive oil
- 5 drops Lavender oil
- 10 drops Rose oil
- 5 drops Lemon oil

If your puppy needs a quick freshen up, simply rub this blend over their coat and marvel at how great they feel.

BLEND TWENTY FOR FRESH BREATH

- 20 ml. Sweet almond oil
- 6 drops Peppermint
- 8 drops Coriander seed
- 10 drops Cardamom

Use a dropper to give three drops to your dog every day. You will fall in love with the manner in which your pet drools over this blend.

BLEND TWENTY ONE TO EASE TEETHING PAIN

- 20 ml. Sweet almond carrier oil
- 6 drops Myrrh essential oil
- 4 drops Roman Chamomile
- 20 drops Clove bud infusion

You could add several drops of this blend onto a frozen puppy toy, so that they can chew and relieve themselves, as they play with the toy.

BLEND TWENTY TWO TO TREAT ANXIETY AND FEAR

- 20 ml. Sweet almond essential oil
- 1 drop Neroli essential oil
- 2 drop Sweet Basil essential oil
- 8 drops Petitgrain essential oil
- 2 drops Ylang Ylang essential oil
- 6 drops Bergamot essential oil

Just use a few drops of this essential oil as you leave for work and this will take care of the separation anxiety in your pet.

BLEND TWENTY THREE TO TREAT CONGESTION

- 15 ml. Sweet almond base oil
- 5 drops Eucalyptus essential oil
- 5 drops Myrrh essential oil
- 5 drops Ravensare essential oil

The above mentioned blend must be used in a nebulizing diffuser, five to ten minutes at a time for at least four times in a day.

BLEND TWENTY FOUR TO STRENGTHEN THE IMMUNE SYSTEM IN YOUR DOG

The below mentioned blend must be massaged to the dogs neck and chest every day. Use only 2-4 drops of the oil and store the blend in a dark colored glass bottle.

- 15 ml. Sweet almond carrier oil
- 2 drops Ravensare essential oil
- 2 drops Thyme essential oil
- 2 drops Coriander seed essential oil
- 2 drops Niaouli essential oil
- 2 drops Eucalyptus essential oil
- 2 drops Bay Laurel essential oil

BLEND TWENTY FIVE FIRST AID ESSENTIAL HEALING SALVE

The below mentioned recipe will make 4 oz. of salve:

- Olive oil: 1 oz.
- Sweet Almond oil: 1 oz.
- Hazelnut oil: 1 oz.
- Sunflower oil: 1 oz.
- Beeswax: ½ oz.

In order to prepare this salve, you must heat all base oils with the beeswax over gentle heat. Once the beeswax has melted, add 20 drops of vitamin E oil as this is a natural antioxidant.

Allow this to cool for five minutes and add the below mentioned essential oil blend:

- 6 drops Ravensare essential oil
- 5 drops Geranium essential oil
- 2 drops Helichrysum essential oil
- 5 drops Lavender essential oil
- 3 drops Labdunum essential oil
- 5 drops Rosewood essential oil
- 5 drops Thyme essential oil

Mix well and pour into a dark colored glass jar once it cools down completely. In order to elevate the therapeutic value of the base oils, you can infuse them with rose petals, calendula petals, lavender flowers, chamomile flowers and other herbs of your choice.

BLEND TWENTY SIX FOR SKIN ALLERGIES

- 6 drops Lavender essential oil
- 2 drops Carrot Seed essential oil
- 1 drop Roman Chamomile essential oil
- 2 drops Geranium essential oil
- 6 drops Rosewood essential oil
- 1 tbsp. Oatmeal (finely ground)

Mix this blend in 8oz. of all natural shampoo and heal your pet of skin allergies.

BLEND TWENTY SEVEN FOR SKIN INFECTIONS

Take 8 oz. of the all-natural shampoo base that you can create based on the recipe mentioned in the later part of the book and add the following essential oils to heal your dog from skin infections and minor wounds:

- 2 drops Labdunum essential oil
- 1 drop Helichrysum essential oil
- 4 drops Ravensare essential oil
- 3 drops Lavender essential oil

BLEND TWENTY EIGHT FOR COAT CARE

- 2 drops Grapefruit seed extract
- 4 drops of Rosemary

Use this blend in your dog's all natural shampoo to witness a soft and smooth fur.

BLEND TWENTY NINE FOR INCREASING APPETITE

- 2 drops ginger
- 4 drops lemon
- 2 drops cardamom
- 1 drop spearmint

Use this blend over your dog's paws and notice them drool over it. Using it twice a day can help in yielding results in a week's time.

BLEND THIRTY FOR EYESIGHT

- 15 ml. of Sweet almond oil
- 2 drops Rosemary
- 2 drops Cypress
- 4 drops Frankincense

This is an amazing blend to facilitate improvement of eyesight in your elderly dog.

THE ALL NATURAL DECYL POLYGLUCOSE SHAMPOO BASE

This all natural decyl polyglucose shampoo base is a great solution for the grooming that your dog needs. It is extremely gentle and generously foaming.

The recipe provided here will make around 8oz. of shampoo base and you can add your dog's favorite essential oils to it, depending on the reason for which you are creating the blend. You can also infuse your water with herbs such as horsetail, nettles, marshmallow root, slippery elm, chamomile flowers, etc. This elevates the therapeutic value of the blend.

- *Distilled water: 4.5 oz.*
- *Decyl Polyglucose: 3.2 oz.*
- *Cider Vinegar: ½ tsp.*
- *Xanthan Gum Powder: ½ tsp.*
- *Rosemary Antioxidant Extract: 1 ml.*
- *Grapefruit Seed Extract: 1ml.*

You must use hot water for creating these blends – it helps the herbs and other ingredients blend well. Add all ingredients except the xanthan gum powder once your herbs are infused. The xanthan gum powder goes in once all other ingredients are blended together. Blend well and add the essential oils based on your requirement.

This shampoo base can be used in all recipes where we want to use an all-natural shampoo.

All recipes provided in this book are safe and harmless. I sincerely hope that you are able to draw benefits using these recipes and help your pets stay happy and healthy.